Hermes in the Kitchen Drawer
and Other Poems

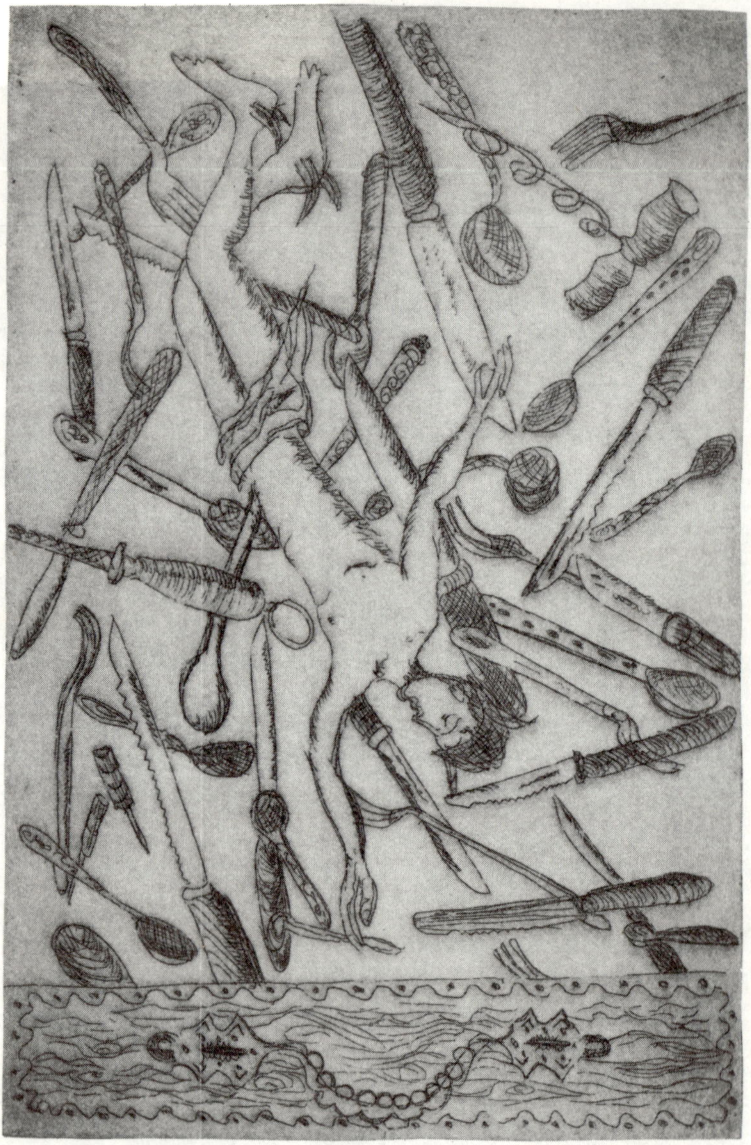

Alan Bleakley

Hermes
in the Kitchen Drawer
and Other Poems

Gateway Books, Bath

First published in 1990
by Gateway Books
The Hollies, Wellow,
Bath, BA2 8QJ

© 1990 Alan Bleakley

No part of this book may be reproduced
in any form without permission from
the publisher, except for the quotation
of brief passages in criticism

Cover photo by Sue Bleakley and Dee Hirtenstein
Frontispiece by Sue Bleakley
Set in 10½pt on 12½ Joanna
by Bryan Williamson, Darwen, Lancs.
Printed and bound by BPCC Wheatons Ltd
of Exeter

British Library Cataloguing in Publication Data:
Bleakley, Alan
 Hermes in the kitchen drawer : and other poems.
 I. Title
 821.914

ISBN 0-946551-61-8

Acknowledgements

Some of these poems first appeared in:
Arvon Foundation anthology; Bananas; Cornwall in Verse
anthology; London Review of Books; Manhattan Review;
New Poetry; Orbis; South West Review; South West
Review anthology; Stand; The Honest Ulsterman;
Times Literary Supplement; Transformation –
Poetry of Spiritual Consciousness anthology; Westwords.

"The world is presence and not force.
Presence is not mind.

...
It fills the being before the mind can think."

(From "St. John and the Back-Ache" by *Wallace Stevens*).

This collection is dedicated to Sue, Phaedra, Brioney and Sam.

Thankyou to Peter Redgrove.

Contents

I Family

Fertility Rites	3
At the Bedside	4
I Dreamed That My Mother Died, Suddenly, While Caught in a Thunderstorm	7
The Wheat in Ferment	8
Fishing With My Father	9
My Father's Water Cure	10
Reparation (I dream of my father)	11
Earwigging	12
Half and Half and the Animal Third	15
History of the Solar Plexus	16
Grandmother	17
Holomovement	19
Swimming	21
Cleaning Out the Fish Pond	22
The Imagination of Air	23
Industry	24

II Mythology (Cerridwen's Smile After the Deluge)

Sphinx	29
The Three Marys	30
The Healer's Art	31
The Fourth Heaven	33
Hermes in the Kitchen Drawer	35
The Slaughterhouse Tour	36
Delivery	38
A Thin-skinned Hero	39
Woman Asleep in a Churchyard	41
Medusa	42
Calling Song	44

The Apple Fall and the World Orchard	45
The Water Charm	46
Gloriana (Heart of the Oak)	47
Would Christ Eat Cape Fruit?	48
Awareness Through Posture	49
Fish-gutters Sunk Into the Rhythm of Work	50

III Nature

At the Reptile House (Regent's Park Zoo)	55
Three Rounds With Winter	59
Son and Daughter to the Cow	60
Tree Lore	62
Patrick Henry Mall	65
Stony Littleton Longbarrow	67
Newquay: The River Gannel	70
Sailors' Dreamspeak	71
Seafarers	72
Storm-fish	73
The Sea Reclaims	74
Specimens in Resin, Specimens in Cases	75
The Storm That Hoodwinks	76
Devolution of Light	77
Dream-work	80
Ordinary Things, Once Discovered Never Forgotten	81
Wintering	82
Bone Augury	83
Tremedda Farm	84

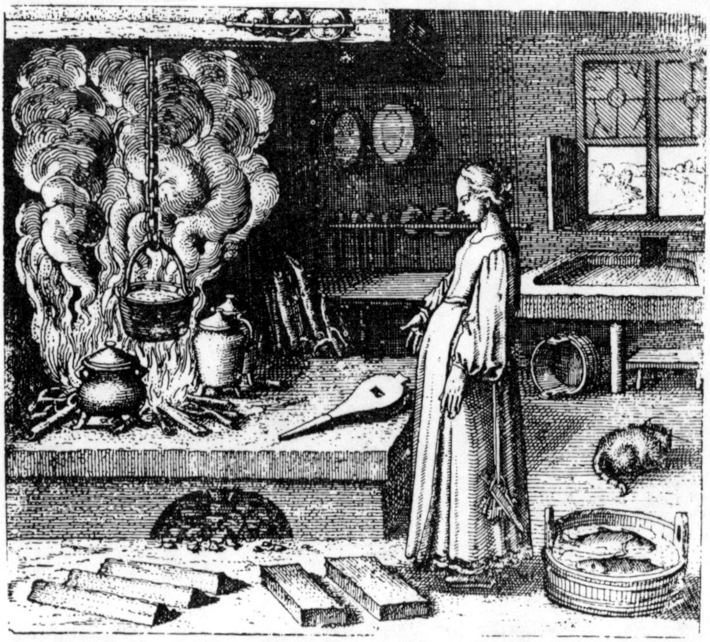

Part I
Family

Fertility Rites

The lady with the red hair wears a red fur
Around her neck, a dead fox.

She muscled me into this world
From between her legs (my first blooding).

My mother's smell is like the musk of the fox.
I grow to love the always-warm pelt –

The fox becomes my familiar.
I flesh the fur and raise it to life.

I give him two penetrating
Eyes, and pristine teeth.

It is March, and I have grown to manhood.
Rain pips the waxy evergreens

By the roadside, where I find the stiff corpse
Of a young fox, fur glossed by the rainfall.

Hardened blood lips the clean white enamel
Of the incisors; one eye is good,

The other closed by matter as hard as resin.
I lift him to look into his good eye.

He has that familiar smell.

At the Bedside

(For my late mother, student of the Rose and Cross)

I

Standing at the bedside
Of my dying mother
I see for a moment
What I take to be snow
Falling onto her bandaged head,
And hear the voice of my
Long-dead father
Whispering to her
Through the falling powder.

II

The Mysterium: the Doves of Diana
Descending like snow, which is also
The Ka-soul rising,
The rested ghost unwrapping
From her body, first ascending,
Then falling as a light rain
Wrought into powder as it passes
Through the chill of her aura,
Settling about her yellowed skin
And the crisp, laundered cotton.

There is no immortality, but
Eternal Presence.

III

She is singing to herself
And we cannot hear it –
We are already diseased by her absence.

Now she wears a headdress of dry snow;
The voice of my father

Still whispers about the bed.
The bandage turbanning her
Shaven head brightens like phosphor.

Her singing rises above
The forced breath and suddenly
The coldness around her stands distinct,
Ringing out two feet from her skin,
And for a moment
The bed linen audibly crackles
While the vault of the ward
Seems to fill with attracted thunder
That has rolled through
Each ice-bright windowpane
And has mingled in its passage
With my mother's rising voices.

From this mixing of weathers,
A sweet smell unfolds
That spills into my clothes,
Resisting the background odours
Of lint, chlorine and laundered linen.

At this moment everything
Is in surreal and absolute focus –
Death is crisp.

Then just as suddenly
The ward seems to jerk back
To a scratchy somnambulism,
Patients adjusting for sleep
Against the sour taunt of bed-sores,
Nurses going about their business
With reflex certainty.

I touch my mother one last time, tenderly
Confirming the welcome, contagious smell
Of her parting, that is exactly

The smell of fern after heavy rain,
Which I pass on silently to family
Gathered at the bedside, heads hung.

IV
Even when she is boxed in pine
I catch that smell – amongst the folds
Of my shirt, the rills and whorls of my skin.

Her fingers first caught that after-storm
Smell from the plants she loved,
Where it lingered in the sweet gums of split stems,
In mucus raised from the pores of resting leaves,
And even in the moisture of root-hairs
From the composted weed.

V
This fresh odour, that curled out
With her Ka-soul, fell as snow,
And raised a concentrated thunder,
Has wound into the water-course
Of my membranes;

Not immortal, but eternally present
Mother-familiar; ancient
Smell of fern; journeying
At the far end of her dream.

No pine box can contain her current,
Even her Remains were returned
To the courses of the Atlantic sea –

A crisped flower spread wide,
Soaking back its waters.

I Dreamed That My Mother Died, Suddenly, While Caught in a Thunderstorm

Do you see? She drops
Like a moth at the flame.

What weather for her death!
Rolling thunder; the taste

Of electricity
As if our tongues touched

The silvered anode of the storm-battery.
I watch her sudden drop

Onto the black earth
Leaving her body-print

That the rain waits to enter.
The wind stitches a new body

Out of shining water,
While she sinks into the mud

Quivering under the thunder.

The Wheat in Ferment

The wheat in ferment.
It seemed that way to me,
A strange high wind in August
Whipping across the ripe heads,
Followed by bulging rainclouds
From the west Atlantic
Opening themselves
To bruise the full beads of grain.

Mixture of wind, rain and wheat
Conjured the smell that drowned
All others, and through its pungency
Came a memory of childhood,
Of a dash through a wide field
Rippling with near-bursting grain,
Chest-high, my outstretched hands
Just brushing the whiskery tips
In haste, before the darkening
Sky split open and a mass of rain
Hooped around us,
My mother ahead
Urging me to hurry.

At home, we stood in our
Wet clothes before an open fire
Laughing at the plume of steam
Rising from my trousers
Turning stiff as card,
And the rich wheat smell
Poured from my mother's hair
As she knelt to comb
The wetness out before the fire,
Thin straws of amber stalk
Clinging to her black cotton dress.

Fishing With My Father

The luminescence of the sea's wastes

A boat's wake by night
A brilliant scud on an oily sea

The pressing darkness like a bandana,
Making us work for our breath.

The banditry of the sea's silver-skinned fruits

Everything proteinous moving, vigilant,
The water a black mirror sliced

By two lines from the stern,
Suddenly fiery with detritus.

When the stern-lines' hum switches
To a jitter, we pull in

A dozen or so mackerel,
Carelessly tossed towards a bucket

Their tails slapping at the thick plastic
Our fingers slimy with spent scales.

The waters always threatening
To unpack a mystery

And tonight, I have the ready tonic
Of youth, and a patient father.

My Father's Water Cure

The body a cask, a vat;
The still, ghostly sperm in the
Tub of the body, rested.

A newly-dead man boxed in
Pine, the resting sperm ready
For the flames; the dark innards

Have voiced down their verses at death
And the thin wood has drawn to
Its grain the last murmurs of

The material man, which
It will sing into red flame.
When the dust settles and is

Gathered, it will be scattered
Over a piece of humping sea,
A small patch of green water

Whitened by ash which the current
Rakes out to the fringes of
A resting barrel of rock that

Has for aeons soaked up the
Man overturned by disease
And cured him entirely.

Reparation
(I dream of my father)

My long-dead father comes to me
Under black wraps, talking
Familiar clipped Glaswegian,
Comes close with beery breath, asking
For the loving conversation
We never had, after youth's piping
Blood had swept me from out of his shadow
And I wanted to shout down
His strained Victorian values.

Now I wish that I could lift the cap
From this enclosed sleep and bend
To kiss his head, a tangle
Of black hair rinsed in sea-spray.
I might walk out of this dream
And catch him smoking by the window,
Ready to wake me before light
To go fishing for conger or shark
And share a salty joke, between men.

Earwigging

A thunderous argument
Between my parents
In the room next to mine
And I am animal, bristling,
Nervous, hair hurting at the root;
Most of all, my eardrums are at the point
Of bursting, so charged that I can hear
The dust settle in the uncertain silence
That follows the bitching.

The hurt ear, straining.
The youth's ear turned crimson
Running hot with the soaked-up
Sex moans of parents making up.

Freud was wrong – the primal scene
Is not scotopic but aural.
The lost erogenous zone
Is the embryo-shaped ear
With its delicate inscape
Of drumhead, ringing bone
And Lilliputian canals
Singing with the fluids
That keep us upright
In the face of gravity.

I never saw my parents making love
But heard them often, and suffered
Both the thunder and whine
Of their late night rows
When dad came home drunk and demanding.
I strained to hear the tenor of their words,
Hoping, I suppose that the listening ear
Might be healing, even at a distance,

Even if unknown or ignored.
I was always relieved to fall away
From the tension into sleep,
And wake to the sound of outdoors, of rain
On the roof and the rushing gutters
Free from human talk and war of words.

We have shifted libido
From the ears, now cloyed with cocktail talk,
Or thickened insensibly through a history
Of fending off sprays of rancorous comment.
We cannot sustain listening,
Appreciate the erotic charge of silence,
Or hear through to the underbelly
Of words, where repressed outrage clings.
We cannot bear to listen to our own failings
Yet swill gossip like a mouthwash
And spit this out as conversation.

The raging ear poisoned like Hamlet's
In a rising heat of chatter within the family,
That is applied directly to the earwax,
Loved ones dripping barbed comment
Which is to say, while your back is turned,
So that canals are stripped bare by flagellant speech,
Slender bones fall away from their duty
Bleached by caustic comment.
Drums are perforated by thorny jibes
And hearing finally dissolves
Amongst the voices of strangers
One's own diction murdered by family
Talking at table, with barbarous intent.

Coda

The dead return to haunt our talk
And we let them dominate our conversation,
Maligned ghosts eavesdropping at the after-funeral

Discussions and the reading of the Will,
Talking directly into our heads
As conscience and guilt.
We poison their ears over and over
Cursing them for reminding us
That we never did our best for them,
That we could have done more,
That if they were still alive we would
Make up for lost conversation.

But how can we talk this way
When we have forgotten how to listen,
How to ease the sprain in others' words
And slip the knots of intimate conversation.
We no longer spend comfortable time
With the chattering aspen;
Or uncomfortable, catching the screech
Of winter winds through stripped trees,
Like the howlings of Ariel from the ungaped pine.
Rather, we are glued to the characterless
Noise of everyday clamour: supermarket muzak,
And the pale scripts of soap operas.

How can the ear register pleasure
When our coffins are swallowed
Into the belly of the crematorium
To insipid piped music, instead of the shared
Eversion of our hurting gut
In a fiery public wailing?

Half and Half and the Animal Third

Her wound opens with clock precision.
There is animal life in the turning blood.
She is the May-Queen crowned,
Both the mistress of the hunt
And the animal
That will be brought down and skinned.

She is deer-skinned, badger-clawed, prescient.
Has the same knowledge of the rivers
As the spawning trout.

She burrows in the rank earth
To reconstitute ancestral bones,
Pulling on the colours
Of the turned soil as she goes.

When she visits the city,
The streets turn up their tarmac
In thick pleats so that she might
Snuffle at the dirt beneath.

Her changes telegraph
To every beast within her circle,
Almost half the world
Bleeding at any one time.
The other half – men of science –
Dissecting animals while they still live,
Mopping up the blood with their shirt-tails.

History of the Solar Plexus

My grandfather was a butcher
Who'd show me how to split the belly
Of a rabbit, and clean out the guts
With firm cuts through the pearly fascia.

After the plum-red tracery of blood
Had been wiped from the marble top,
With a sure stroke he'd dock the bob-tail
And brush the fine hair across my cheeks.

But my stomach would knot as he scuffed
The sawdust floor and raised the trapped smell of old
    blood,
And my eye would wander to the day's row of rabbits,
Skinned, and hung by their mouths on plain steel hooks.

Grandmother

My grandmother smelt of camphor.
Her rooms smelt of camphor.

Her furniture grew a skin
Of grey dust that trapped the smell
And incubated an even more pungent odour.

Moths with paper wings lay dead
In the camphor-caskets:
The sombre kitchen dresser
And the dark oak bedroom wardrobe
Stuffed with wedding lace,
Reeking with the sharp oil.

As she aged, my grandmother's face
Adopted a mask close to
The colour of the camphor balls,
But waxy to the touch.

A magpie, hoarder like herself,
Would come and tap on the
Leaded window-panes
For scraps of bacon fat.
Sometimes I would offer
The twists of white rind
To the greedy bird
And think of her pallid skin
As the fat greased my fingers.

Before she died
She forsook the magpie,
Telling me that a robin
Would come to her window
As a sign of her death,
And that she would echo
The blood-badge of its chest.

Holomovement
(For Sue)

(The apple-seed, a memory of the whole tree)
Round-headed sperm in wet millions, manifest.

The ovum excites. At fertilisation
The tissue walls of the enormous cell electrify,

Mitochondria fizzing with the passage of oxygen
And protein mosaics reformulating

As nucleic acids cluster, jiggling,
And a calcium holocaust erupts –

A white, granular cloudburst, the cell,
Weather-dense, storms into repeated division.

The embryo grows, in-pouring skin
That evolves as delicate, shiny gut;

The middle tissue forms the first muscle, as thin
As cellophane, that includes the rippling transparent heart;

And, for a while, there are primitive gills gently
Feathering with the rhythms of the thin brine of the
     womb.

Womb sac, an open eye and ear to light and sound,
To changing wavelength, to the clear pulse

Of the mother's blood through the thin umbilicus,
And the deep, regular echo of her heartbeat.

The embryo grows negentropically,
Energy into matter, wave and particle manifest.

The newborn unfolds to air encased in a
Buttery vernix and a hardening tracery of blood –

A memory-membrane beneath which his skin
Enfolds to tiny, shimmering gut villi, fingers

Across which shining food slips, protein polishing
    protein,
The variously-coloured milk of the mother sucked deep,

Drawn inside, like an arcing, sustenant rainbow.
The mother's milk is coloured by her whole current.

The baby shits from its bright gut as it is born,
Mingling this with the mother's blood such that

Sustenance and excrement are mirrored as equally-valued
    aspects
Of the same movement, common inspiratrix.

The rotating head guides the body at birth, the child
Hauling behind him the irridescent placenta on belly-
    string,

The second birth – a resurrected body,
A second coming; expelled yolk, oily and nutritious.

The mother's interior light made plain, a holomovement,
Unfoldment complete as the navel is tied, then

Boy rolls off the glistening
Belly of the mother, refracting light,

Inspired by gravity; baby and mother breathing in rounds.
Light manifesting on each round of breath.

The apple-seed, a memory of the whole tree.

Swimming

We are re-made in a round
Mirror of water, assembling
And dis-assembling at will.
A high cloud steps back,
The sun moves through us
And hits the water, shifting
Opacity to transparency,
Revealing a torrent of small
Silver fish into whose
Trembling gills the sky
Has collapsed whole,
Is eyebright and lipgloss
For these creatures who have
Fallen into the paradise
Of Davy Jones' open box.

My daughter folds into the water
To relieve an issued hairshirt
Of eczema, treating same with same,
Prickly rash by salt-burn,
Returning her itch
To the round of rubbing water.

She surfaces through the froth
Of her dive – Aphrodite
With eyeliner – eyes pencilled
With Proserpine's coal
To see better in the undersea dark
And for the boys to better see
Her darkness, by which means
She will in time effect a skin cure.

Cleaning Out the Fish Pond

She is folded upon herself,
Kneeling to meet the muscle
Of the frog as it tries to leap,
When her hands trap it under
The belly, and lift it
Clear of the mud
Smoothed to the bowl
Of the fish pond
Below the hanging willow.

The frog eyes her through a film
Of mucus, and sees nothing,
For she makes no sharp movements
But gently drops him into
A bed of glistening leaf-mould.

There are a dozen more
Wintering in the thick ooze,
Motionless, as if suspended
In aspic, until the skin
Of her fingers runs across
The smooth humps of their backs.

She is tempted to try their cool skin
Against her January-chapped lips.

The Imagination of Air

When the picture is going well
The artist has the smell
Of the sea about her;
Or what is left on shells
When the tide has passed,
And what is given off
From the popped vesicles
Of nearly-dried bladder wrack.

It is the smell that
Goes into the composition
And gives it serenity.
Before that, when the picture
Is stilted, there is lead in her hands,
A poison of thick air,
The smell of old water;

And the paint slips off the brush
Like egg yolk, shying at the canvas,
Malodorous oils slippery as liver,
Lumping and sloping, her fingers
Angrily picking at the pigment.

This is when the imagination of air
Is bigger than the hand that greets it.

Industry

A Victorian pension paid in iron bars;
A wedlock to rooms cast from metal,
The long-term committed tapping over and over

On the grilles of asylum windows
Raising blood on split knuckles and rancour
From warders who spill ringing bunches of keys

From their middles; whose marriages are rusted out,
Who are wasting to the toothless suck of bad blood,
Iron drained from the slippery platelets,

Vinegar running through them instead of blood,
The once red flesh of Adam
Dismantling itself from within.

The core drained white returning
To the oldest condition of earth.

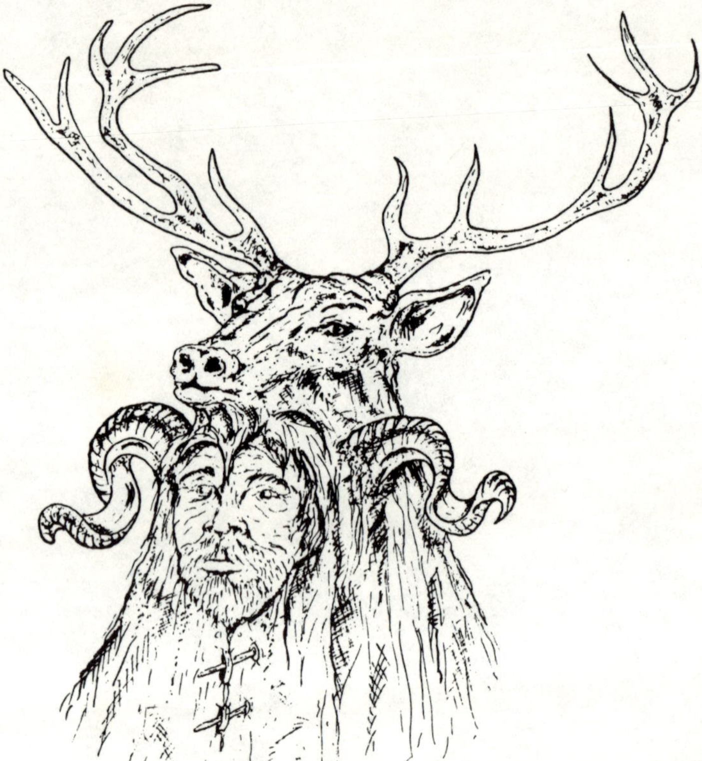

Part II
Mythology

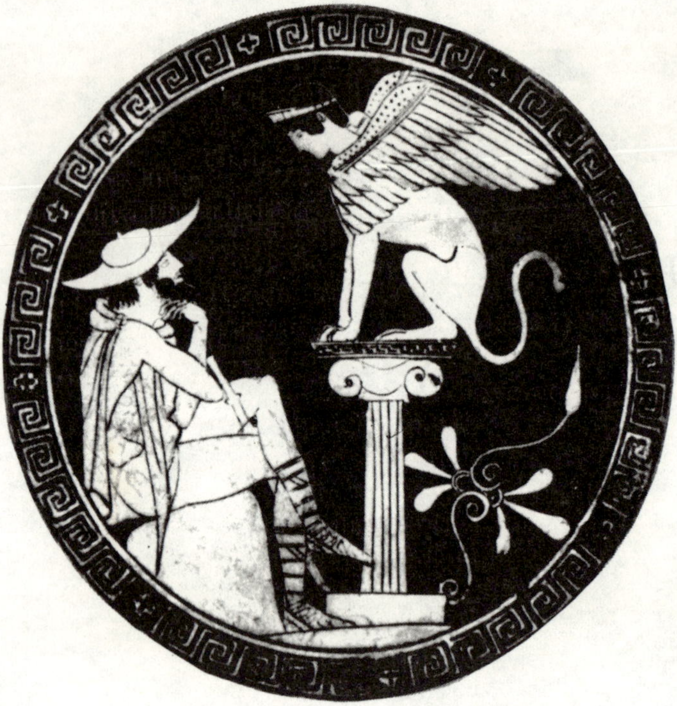

Sphinx

Why is the Sphinx woman in front and animal behind? Because the back-side of the sky that is the northern arc never receives the drowning light of the sun or moon but is lit by the ancient stars and is said to represent the way of the animal powers, the intelligence of the heart. "Sphinx" and "sphincter" have the same root, which is "to bind tight" – the Sphinx was also called "the throttler" – what binds tight at the crown of the northern sky is the Great Bear star-form that circles the still point of the Pole, the perceived centre of the universe. In its annual revolution, the bear never dips below the horizon, and so was thought to be bound to the centre of the firmament: a mother always protecting her child that is the Little Bear whose tail-tip is the centre of the world. This indicated resolution, commitment and dependability, the Mother Bear the source of all things, both fount of birth and receiver of all souls at bodily death. The Egyptians called her the Mother-of-the-Field-of-Heavens; also, the Mother-of-Beginnings. She was the water cow – the hippopotamus. To the Celts she was Ked or Keridwen, the cauldron or womb of creation.

So how can God be a man, when the Mother births all? Or should matrix and patrix be co-equal in creation? Creation stories were invented by men itching to relieve themselves of the animal cloak, of the reverberating circuits of the brain's kernel, of the indignity of the actual descent from the lungfish and the stinking mudhopper, a stutter in evolution where gill became lung. But this turn beckoned the masculine spirit that is breath rather than the bright waters of the womb, where at one time, each of us sports primitive gills and breathes against the grain of Nature. With this turn to air came the dangers of inflation, of ballooning up in pride and dominance, as our first breath puffed up those spongy sacs, bringing with it the illusion of nobility, though our bodies still dragged in the mud, which, billions of years on, is the common ground for human pride.

The Three Marys

The sky is pegged back
By falling waters.

Say Hail! to the three Marys:
Mother, anointer and whore,

Who wrap into the mascara
Of streetwalkers, so that

The coal is dissolved and runs
In tears the colour of bruising

Over skin that has been palmed
Yard over yard by needy men.

These same men are driven
By the old-brain animals

That live at the back of the wind,
At the underside

Of the thunderheads, where
They conspire to dream the three Marys

Back into the bellies
Of sow, bitch and she-wolf.

The Healer's Art

A royal flush of revived spirits.
A hand packed with the metaxy
Of ghosts and familiars,
Good weather at the fingertips.

She deals a winning hand
Into the leaden skies
That depress the movement
Of joint and ligament.
She makes a pass and the sun
Breaks through; she palms the pain
And brings out the true grain of the hurt.
She has a lightning-crackle
About her own skin that jumps
Through the deadened gristle, so that
The joint once more feels its spring.

And the unwelcome ghost that slips
From the shivering man
As the surfacing sulphur
Of a fever, is touched
In a royal handshake.

The ghost turns to momentary
Egg-white in her fiery palm,
And is gobbled by the salts
Issuing from her fingers.

Then she shakes hands with herself
Under running water,
And the spirit of the fever
Is stitched into the rainfall
That has run through the healing
Copper of the plumbing,
Meeting with the other rivers
Of the town's flushed garbage –
A confluence of unwanted ghosts
Pulled out to deepest sea.

The Fourth Heaven

The first heaven is silence;
Then came the funiculus,
The raw stomach and the reflex
Of the grasping hand

Within the second heaven
That is the celestial waters,
The unstirred brine resting
With the tears of the embryo.

The third heaven is the seven steps
To the blue north pole
Which is the star-stuff,
The distant, untouchable brimstone
Of the bright bear *Ursa Major*
In her annual revolution.

The seven stars have descended
As the subtle body
That is halo to flesh and bone.

In the embryonic state
The juices of the forming glands
Wash through the shining body
To shape the guardian animal
Animating the spreading tissues
And settling into features,
So that the child is born round sow,
Dreamy she-bear, nervous
Red-bristled fox, obstinate mule,
Ravenous mink, scavenging gull,

Animal given with the babe
Born into the fourth heaven,
That is the four quarters of Earth,
Where the child recognises
Its habitat in the damp earth-smells
Of the friendly burrow or lair;

The familiar rub of woodskin
In the high sanctuary
Of the beamed tree-house;
And the taste of ancient salt
Rising from the scuffed silica
Of the vaulted beach cave.

Hermes in the Kitchen Drawer

Hermes in the kitchen drawer
As crackling silver foil;
As the serrated meat-knife
And silvered electric slicer
That polish themselves on gristle.

Hermes as the gleaming
Mirror-backs of spoons
Into which the polisher reads
Whatever she wishes.

And with the help of the polished god
Is led into reverie
Away from the sentinels of the dinner service
In the beize-lined case

To a disorder of hungry gods –
Ill-tempered Chronos chewing on his children,
Hercules forking appetising horseshit,
Ugly Hephaestus busily tempering blades;

Olympus entirely silvered with upset cutlery;
The polisher, ravenous.

The Slaughterhouse Tour

(Students on introductory Catering courses tour a slaughterhouse as part of the curriculum).

The manager of the slaughterhouse
Pulls on a Havana wrap;
Stored sunlight of Cuba gently fires his lungs
Warming the alveoli with the soft winds of Pinar del Rio.

He displays a collection of hanging stiffs,
A library of red meats catalogued by steel hook,
Each carcass an unread book hinged on bone,
The leaves of muscle glued by frozen fat.

The visitors are also stiffening
At the sheer volume of motionless protein;
At the smell of hot tobacco
Mixed with the sickly-sweet of dry fat.

Their bodies recognise a ritual
Both sinister and sexual
Aroused by the bizarre parade of meat,
For this visit perhaps stirs a root memory

Of the ancient initiation
Of the taurobolium,
Where the young aspirant, standing in a pit
Beneath a slaughtered bull, is showered with blood.

But on this tour the animals are frozen,
Their blood already drained,
The taurobolium lost to another age
When it had meaning as a restimulation

Of the youth's own birth: a hot impress
Of the mother's pelvis on the face.
These visitors are reminded
Not of the mother's blood at birth

Which has been blanched out by our culture,
But of the distant smell
Of the father's celebration cigar.
Then the slaughterhouse manager

Is seen as a kindly man, a father-feeder,
Forgiven, like the men who surround us at birth
Where there is also a moment of freezing
As the umbilicus is unceremoniously snipped

And we are born into a circle of Fathers.

Delivery

Against the chilling white light
Stretched across the whole sky,
A dog-fox barks at dead of night.
The foetus, passing full-term,

Turns between rolls of thunder
As if to smell the cauterised
Heart-wood of a lightning-struck oak,
And adjusts for delivery.

She feels her belly's final stretch,
Thunder barks then spills, as the gut
Of the weather delivers itself
Dragging with it the smell

Of split oak smouldering.
The child tugs at its rooted cord
And turns again, fully seasoned
In the fluids of the mother

Who will unbutton to the world
A boy named Dances-Like-Trees,
An oak-king born to the delivery-drum of thunder;
Small morris-man shirted and trousered in white sap

Hears thunder on delivery and adjusts his red crown,
Kicks off his bloody garters, sings
To the world, rests on her wet belly
Fingers reaching

Like a sapling's tender boughs tapping at the damp sky.

A Thin-skinned Hero
(Heart disease resulting from stress is the modern Plague)

A child discards boyhood
Swings up from the sow's tits
Is bearded by the pig-mother's milk

And smiles, rippling muscle.
As he rises from the animal's underbelly
Blood rushes to his head

And stiffens his penis simultaneously.
All his life he will look
To the two blood-rivers turning within,

Both of luminous waters, running
Until his Circle of Destiny is complete.
Then an indoor thunderstorm will rage

With its ringing-down fingers
Of shock-white lightning –
Silver-handed lymphocytes

Irradiated by the heart-star will race
Too late to save the punctured life,
And the plasma's brilliant smell will be dulled

To that of hay stored wet.
The five-limbed star of the outer senses
Will sink in a tub of blood

To join the dark lianas of hanging intestine
Strung on sheets of tissue as beautiful as silk,
Tearing under gravity, while blood rains

Through a closed fist of muscle,
Sweeps around the slippery cavity of the chest,
And the hero marks the thunder of a burst heart.

As surely as the cloudburst,
The hero falls to earth and drenches it with his fluids.
Now music-making clean bones will appear in time to
    swell

Under the primitive bandaging of red mud,
And fall out of the body
To be combed by a deafening under-earth wind.

Woman Asleep in a Churchyard

A black yew bowing to a crypt.
She has visited the vault
That smells like a mushroom farm

And now walks up to daylight
Only to descend to sleep
Under the arch of the yew.

As she steps into dreaming
Ancestors buttoned up in stone
Peel out of their tombs

To squeeze up the yew's roots
And shower from the buds as bright ghosts
Walking into the woman's sleep.

They surface carrying a deathly dew –
A wash of otherworld spittle
Soaking the dry-as-a-wafer dream,

That is an eros unbuttoned
From stone; a water that animates
The figures who stalk her dream

So that the dead refresh the living
By fleshing out the dream
Under the black umbrella of the yew.

Medusa
(Tyrol, 1982)

Water polishing itself in coils
Raises such a shine
That light pours through the rushing river
Like silvered ribbons, flapping
In the current.

The skins of pebbles lining the riverbed
Have been polished off as shining streamers
Winding into the riverlight,
Stripped by the violent water
Which peels and gathers the information of stone
That is distributed downstream
By the servicing current.

A woman walking the ravine
Stops by the river's edge, caught in such a way
Amongst the dappled shadows of firs
That for a moment she seems to fragment
Into windblown streamers treated by sunlight,
Her information confused in the dance
Between a shifting body of light and its shadow.

She walks on, trailing her shadow
Which reverse-polishes the sun-stained riverbank,
Parting sunlight as she moves, in her own shape.
And close by, the shining river-pebbles'
Streamers of unwound stone seem to rise, bleached
On the shafts of sunlight that drill through the dark
Canopy of trees, so that the woman
Is crowned with ringlets of polished air,
The mirror-bright information of stone
That is sharp light cut and drawn from water
Beamed up on sunray as a headdress of shimmering snakes.

The woman seems to grow taller, and at this moment
Turns, fixing me with her stare.
Her coruscating pupils have gathered
Cold light of water, shine of stone,
And a firefly dance of solid air;
The reflecting river unwinding
Into a movement of shadow and light that is organised
Into a single glassy stare seen through
A waterfall of forest lights.

She will turn you into glistening stone with a single look:
Medusa, tall polisher of men.

Calling Song

He calls it magic by the senses
She calls it floating stone.

She calls it whisker on the curve of the world
He calls it solitary pine.

He calls it oak-man in empty-handed combat
She calls it meditation on muscle-sugars.

She calls it secret-nestling-in-filth
He calls it washing-down time.

He calls it nightmare by prescription, a terrible disassembly
She calls it worksong.

She calls it intoned mantra
He calls it swallowed serpent, crying from the belly.

He calls it passage-of-wind song
She calls it the jitterbug waltz.

They call it the signal noise that made murderous Cain.

The Apple Fall and the World Orchard

Here is a polarity in the apple fall –
A cobble of tops glazed by rain
Looking as clean and waxy
As they would in their blue tissue wraps
Selling by the pound.

But kick them over and the rotten halves sing out
With a heady odour of cider,
Pulp under firm top-flesh.

The apple fall mirrors the world divided,
North and south, toned muscular front
And pulpy ferment.

Another month and the apples will be wholly mulch,
Top-frosted by the crisp nor'-easters.

The Water Charm

("*Is getting well ever an art,/ or art a way to get well?*"
– from "Unwanted" by Robert Lowell).

One way to avoid getting well, that is heroic art,
Is to button on the abrasive hair-shirt
That is the itch screaming back at the fingernail,
The overcoat of eczema wrapping the true disease
    beneath:
Symptom suppressing cause.

One way to get well is to take tonic
Standing under a thunderstorm with the eyes rolled up
In contemplation of the skull's underside
Washed in shock-absorbing waters.

Torrents of rain, and the alpha waves of relaxation –
This is water above, lake below:
"Resourceful Thrift" says the I Ching,
The superior man, overcoming the psychosomatic scratch
Through spiritual inquiry,
Believes that there is no itch to scratch
And that he has avoided joining the family of skin-shedders
Who find the grave earlier than most men.

But the inferior serpent
Wound into the hemispheres of the cerebellum
Demands soulful medicine –
Says from the right fork of its tongue, suffer and be wise;
And from the left fork, let healthy folly take its dangerous
    course.

Gloriana (Heart of the Oak)

A river that is thicker than water
Coursing through a valley of fallen trees
Each trunk etched with the royal name: Virgo.

A capillary-tree with Gloriana
At its heart, reaching through families
That flourish because of mixed blood.

And the families of shipwrights are drawn
To the valley of fallen oaks
To impress their trade-names on the trees' flesh.

By axe-blade and saw-tooth the name
Of the royal line is drawn into the bitten oak
And thence into fighting-ships.

Proofed by nail and tar, the mother ship is drawn
Through years of inclement weather
Until the mainmast is rubbed clean of sap,

When the royal ship's planks are torn
One from the other, and the drowned men
Nod to the sea's bed.

Would Christ Eat Cape Fruit?

(For the native peoples of South Africa)

The child-mummy, a boxed
And bandaged boy-Christ
Rolled in lint, wrapped
In the sour-smelling
Ribbons of resurrection
That are both swaddling clothes
And death shroud;

Is the risen Osiris
(Christ born black, out of Africa),

Is born knowing the language
Of fruit: rind, pulp and juice;
Lime wringing out the mouth
In primitive conversation;
Zest of orange, tang of lemon,
Breast milk of the coconut.

The child bearded by dripping pear
Is rocked out of the standing ark
That feeds animals, and brought
To baptismal waters

Where he sees his reflected body
Cradled in the water,
Shining with the clear juice
That has pulled down and held fast
The core of the trumpeting sun.

Awareness Through Posture

The interior Christ is tested
On the tau-cross of
Spine and shoulder-bone.

There he hangs, dark Osiris.
A body of black muscle
Resting on stations of bone,

His head always pitched
To the sinister side,
Christ wrapped into the white tree

That is the skeleton
With its secular crown,
Pulling himself up by the wrists.

Christ's skin blackened by the sun;
His white bones ascending,
Their whereabouts kept secret.

Fish-gutters Sunk Into the Rhythm of Work

Fish-gutters sunk into the rhythm of work
Unhinging purses of muscle with the flick of a knife,
Cannot help but dress themselves in the stripped skins
Of the meat, their oilskins filmed over with fish,
Yellow-clad priests in theriomorphic dress
In the slippery temple of the packing-house.

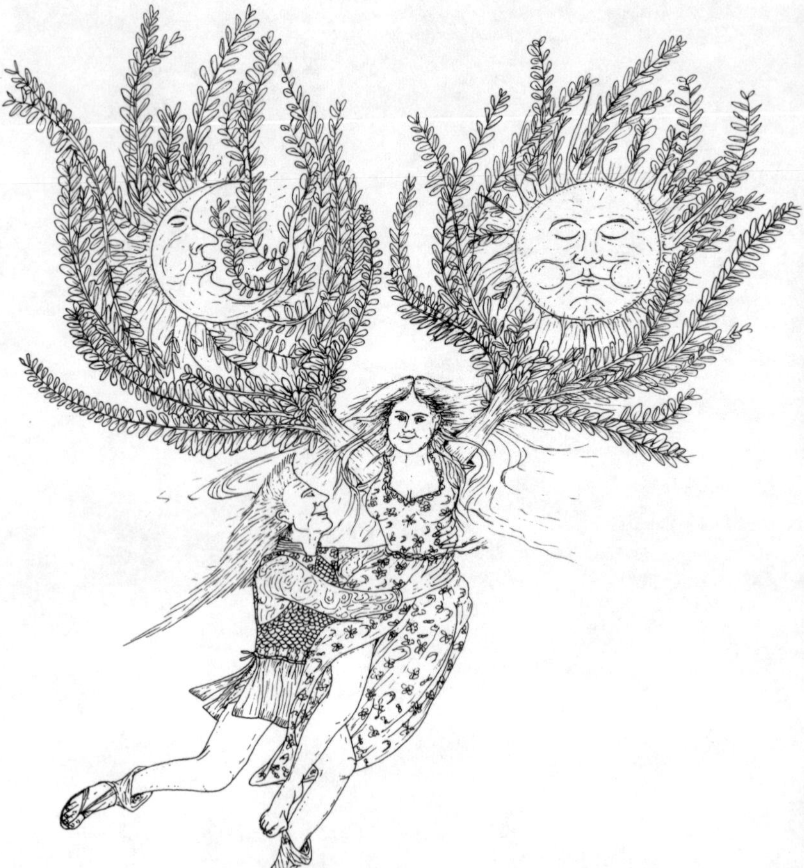

Part III
Nature

At the Reptile House (Regent's Park Zoo)

The damp Jurassic heat of the reptile house
Snakes as thick as your arm
With muscle in rehearsal,
Just one step from being stuffed.

Reptiles boxed behind glass
In a few square feet of ragged desert
Or limp jungle, and we view them limply,
As if they were on the box
In stilted soap-opera with the sound turned off.

Kids palm the thick glass
That separates them from a little piece of Egypt,
But the Nile croc is too slow
For the child's span of attention
And the audience moves on...

Since the crocs don't snap,
The cobras don't spit, rattlers
No longer shake their tails;
The mambas are milked of venom,
Anacondas overcome by torpor,
And sandy chameleons, weary of camouflage,
No longer change, or care for change,
Because predators are long-since stiffs
In the collective memory:
Danger no longer stalks.

Under these antiseptic greenhouse conditions
Mesmeric life has established its presence,
Animals with no need for display forced inward,
Living out the slow, interior life of trance
That is contagious;

That spreads through us as we walk the galleries
Of glazed eyes, so that the mistress of hypnosis
Lopes through the crowd, an Atropos snipping
The ankle tendons of running Time
Until the building itself catches
The substance of the same glassy stare
That is a virus of hitched and enfolded time
Slowing upon itself until the house's biscuit brick
And green glass reclaim themselves as sand.

In this common relaxation
Is a dissolution of barriers.
Amongst the blunt human audience
Who are walking in their sleep,
Snaking through the house in single file and slow step,
The reptiles relish their new-found freedom
And break out of their wraps
To rediscover the knowledge of venom,
The potential of hinged and hanging mandible
And the round dance of muscle
That brings the handshake of death.

The skin of human is now intimate
With the horn of turtle carapace,
Ruff of lizard, close coils of the boa.
There is recognition of a common heritage
From deep within the human,
For the mechanism of the dream is lubricated
With the snake-oil of the brain's ventricles
As the slippery visions
Enter through our reptile nature
That is the stark reality of fight-or-flight:
Panic, and an underbelly of fear.

Humans are afraid of reverie itself
As they are afraid of the snake
Who is the villain

Of our most ancient cultural dream,
And hence source for reverie.

This fear is nudged
By lingering evolutionary shifts
Into a troublesome primate self-awareness
When the snakeskin is shed for hair,
And the soft belly is brought up against the world,
Turned pink by blood running warm
Thrusting us into the animal hunt
Raw to the ready claw of predator,
Shot through with nerves
Mapping the pleasures of face-to-face sex.

The crocodile, bellying out of the primitive glass,
Sniffs out the human pheromones of panic,
Snaps at the genitals of the nearest man,
And, jolted from dream, out flies
The Hero like a Jack-in-the-box,
The original Tarzan ready to crush the croc
And wrestle the rippling python,
Holding back the tide of the dream,
Cold as a fish in the tropical heat,
Standing proud and hairy
Against the smooth-bodied animals,
Replaying the ancient serpent-banishing myth
Of Hercules crushing the poison-spitting Hydra
In her own lair, or George unsettling the dragon,
Cleaving its belly at the mouth of her cave;
Or the man Hermes invading the privacy
Of mating snakes and vitrifying
The shuddering pair, now cast
As the dazzling wonder-working wands
Of the bearded patriarchs;

Or the usurper Zeus slithering
Into Persephone's underearth realm
Disguised as a snake-goddess,

Oblivious to the give-away tuft of wiry hair
Hanging stiff at his chin, larded with black clay.

Or the ganged-up aboriginal men of Arnhem land
Wrestling the trembling, watery rainbowsnake
Out of the sky and into the prison
Of a jealous secret ceremony,
Where the men tell the boys that the snake
Is a symbol of women's menstrual mystery,
Then make the boys bleed to become men,
As a bonding and a forking:
For here they depart not only from youth
But also from equality with girls.
Like the snake's tongue, the sexes part
When they taste the air as they are born
From the mother, and then are cleaved at puberty.
But back at the rump of the tongue's root
We are gulped deep into the common body
Of the serpent, and find the belly
Of the animal genderless, like god.

The hero, that is our rational animal-slaying mind,
Has run up too much credit against the blood-soul,
When the keeper shouts "closing time!"

And I am snatched out of the reverie
And slither out of there
Hanging on to my goose-bumped skin.

The first thing I do as I get outside,
In the moment of blindness
At the smack of yellow light painfully saturating my eyes,
Is to check that my crocodileskin wallet is still nestling
In the back pocket of my jeans –
A reflex I got into the habit of
In the human snake-pit of the city,
Where the low sewers are supposedly inhabited
By reptiles gorged on our wastes.

Three Rounds With Winter

I
The yew's poisonous eyes,
Once soil-bound and silent,
Are pulled into a tangle
Of green hair where they
Will eventually
Shout themselves down from the tree.

II
A robin as dead as Lazarus.
I finger the counterpane of sharp frost
That has been drawn over the bird
In the service of the food chain.
The ice is so cold that it burns;
The bird is in storage, facing heaven.

III
I make great holes in the pond ice,
Disturbing the circle
Of frozen water in which
Fish catch their own reflection.
I fumble in the sharp water
For a catch that refuses my grasp

And will not let me off the hook.

Son and Daughter to the Cow
(South Cadbury)

Rejoicing in the overture
Of mother's muscular tongue
A calf is wrung away
From the red birth wastes.

A tottering young bull
Rises from the earth his home,
The king of slow chlorophyll,
Master of enlarging sap,

Doctor to himself: holly god,
Frost crackling on his skin
In the January chill
As he outgrows a taxis to the soil;

But just as he brings his force
To a point of balance,
He falls face first into butter-thick mud,
Into earth churned by his mother's hooves.

The farmer shouts to his daughter
Whose hands are at another cow's teats
In the milking shed,
Jerking out the last flush

That smacks into the pail,
Which, drawn full from under the belly,
Raises a smile at its centre-waters
As the milk swirls.

The overspills on the concrete floor
Little gashes of milk in the shapes of smiles,
And the maid has the nutritious smile
Of a new mother, as she humps the swilling milk.

Her father shouts over the labouring cow
From whose tattered back end
The calf has been pulled
Spattered with birth jellies and plum-coloured blood.

The farmer slips his arms
Under the belly of the collapsed calf,
And presents the red-haired, muddied beast
To his smiling daughter.

The proud mother turns to smell the red-haired girl.

Tree Lore

I. *Woodland Pharaohs*

An alphabet of trees, guaranteed immortality.

Reading the standing book of the White Poplar,
You can see men bound up in bark-wrap coffins,
Shouting up the sugars to fruiting heads
That quake in the dead still of summer
Speaking springy electrix through their chattering leaves –

Pharaonic imperatives from the lordly Aspen
With her palsied leaves, talking death.

Out of Aspens, men fashion
Measuring-rods for coffin makers.

II. *Lime-tree as Libido*

Placenta oiled with a rainbow
Wet with the birth waters,
A rich meat blessed like the baby,
Buried while the boy suckles
To nourish the roots of a tree
Planted for the mother, a silver Linden.

As this tree grows, so the boy,
His placenta-sister long since withered,
The thick yolk that nourished him in the womb
Drawn into the first rings of growth
Of the four-limbed Lime.

III. Coffins for Sea-folk

Once, all lifeboats were made from trees
So that each rescued man owed his life
To the pitch-soaked planks. The boat,
Like the hollowed log of Osiris,
Offered renewal.

But coffins floated on the seas also
And men knew this by a certain tone
Given off as wood strained against weather,
So that in the call of duty
Some lifeboatmen knew themselves
To be dressing in dead-men's clothes
As they slipped into
The shining waterproofs,
Strapping the sou'westers
Under faces as white as marble,
As cold as the fishmonger's slab.

IV. Kitchen Weddings

In the yard
A butter-drum fashioned from Quickbeam
Churns the milk.
Rowan quickens the lumping of fats;
She is the goddess as butter-bride.

In the larder stands the oak vat
Full of fizzing, honey-brown beer,
A toast to the bridegroom Dionysos
In the pine-timbered temple hung with spider-floss.

Other brides hang in the kitchen, bunched,
Like the fennel, broadcasting licorice;
Little trees of fresh parsley standing proud,
And other herb-wives already promised as garnish
To the red meats tethered for slaughter.

V. *Paper-Birch*

With each supple limb wrapped like a mummy
In loose cylinders of bark, paper-Birch
Speaks for the rebirth of trees
And the weddings between kingdoms.

Patrick Henry Mall
(*A modern shopping centre in Newport News, Virginia*)

A wide ship brimming with interior light
That is a beast becalmed in solid tar,
An animal shaped from recent rock
Whose diet has been wild plants and sappy trees,
Who has processed the green garden of life
Into barren buildings haunted by
The spectres of mutilated trees –

Now raises food at every hour
And flies the flag of free enterprise.

This ship is a paradox: a child that
Eats its greens and asks for more, whose belly,
Running cold with artificial air, is walked
By hungry passengers, wide-eyed from excess of caffeine.

A ship such as this was dubbed with
The mentality of childhood, that wants everything now.
Christened in bubbly, it is a vessel
Of the moment – of the high-flying spirit.
Suitably stocked with sodas, it sails on the winds
Jumped up by a fan of credit cards;
Is fuelled by loose money rubbed roundly
In the unspiritual fat of want
Warmed in the palms of the fortunate;
And heads for the port of the meats of profit –
Large and tender cuts on which the same
Fortunate satisfy a round hunger.

This interior, washed in sodium-white light,
Must not be spoiled by the smell of damp soil
Or animal pelt, and shields its passengers
From the perverse threat of the natural world.

As we walk its polished gangways, styrofoam cup in hand,
We are immune to the thunderheads
That roll over its concrete skin which also bounces back
The voices of the angered gods
Whose collective rage dips down to smack the tarmac
But passes unheard in the antiseptic interior,
With not even a skylight upon which rain could sing,
Or through which moonlight might sneak for a moment
To bless the heads of unsuspecting shoppers.

Stony Littleton Longbarrow
(For *Alick*)

I
A never-ending going down
That stops almost at once

At the sour breath of the long-dead
Who make a greasy water

With their ghostly, noiseless exhalation
Which catches at the cold stone.

II
There is the low light of evening;
A ridgeway of chalk clothed in turf

And the long tomb resting;
A flap of stone under which

The ancients slipped, to nestle
With the skeletons of the dead,

To whisper midwinter sunlight
Into middens of vertebrae.

III
The tomb has a wasp-waist,
Like the womb's neck, where the dead

Slip back noiselessly, while
The restless living come and go

With a murmur, a croaking song
From the throat's root, so that

This under-earth church's passage
Between nave and chancel

Is also a throat, catching
That same frog-song,

The sound caught in the gullet
Like jiggling phlegm

At the point of spit-or-swallow,
For the earth wants to gulp back

And the reflective want to stay
In liminality, in prayer

With the dead, dissolving
Into their supreme darkness.

Then the living can meet
And know the Transparent

In the chamber's closed light,
Who look out at the light

Knowing how the rich feel, buying
Themselves back into the real illumination

That rests in the suffocation
Of pitch, of under-earth oil,

Of black waters running through rock,
The black marrow that gives life.

But the whole lung of the sky,
Issuing the last of the sunlight,

Calls for a spitting-out, for she
Wants also to digest us whole

Until twilight, when the tomb's
Interior is folded out

To greet the descending damp
Of the nightsky which is woven

From the risen skins of the dead,
And is fingered over us now

At the longbarrow's entrance
By a breeze, fresh-sprung from the west.

IV
And the man still sweating at
The deeper cervix of stone

Finds that the suffocating tomb
Is the holding of his own breath

And the damp of the chamber
An issue from his own palms.

So he returns to the entrance
Where a rock is stamped with a fossil.

Here, an ancient sea-snail burst out of itself
At death, so that it could walk

The hanging stone of tombs
And leave its moisture

At the otherwise dry throats,
Greasing the passage of the newly-blind.

Newquay: The River Gannel

The rivermouth has a death-smell
Of rotting shellfish.
On its wide bend, as the moon moves closer,
Big tides pull violently to sea.
Here a man was sucked to death
By his own choice. Perplexed
At the immense quiet that engulfed him
At the point of death,
He furrowed his brow.
At low tide across the width
Of this same rivermouth,
You can see the man's brow echoed
In the neatly-furrowed sand;
Rows of noiseless, soft ribs
Upon which white seabirds perch.

Sailors' Dreamspeak

I
Three boats bobbed in a sea-dance, as partners,
Their sailors sharing dreams of clay-wallowing
On terraces of plum-red earth
After months of the oily Atlantic.

II
The sailors are swayed in their sleep,
The once-cool linen of their bunks now warm
With sweat from shared dreams of the pearly skin
Of their collective lover humping like
A sperm whale choked with musky ambergris.

III
The sailors dream of a tree-rimmed horizon
To replace the pale, unobtruded meniscus
Of the sea, forever lipping threatening skies.

Seafarers

That familiar sucking sea-sound
It root in moon and gravity
Has a killing note
When the westerlies wind to full force.

The sea-boil hisses, as through clenched teeth,
Always the same death sound on this wind,
As if the last issues from the lungs of the drowned
Had so twisted into the patterns of weather

That tape-loops of pneumatic ghosts stranded
Between this world and that
Repeated, unwound, in storm; rested in lull.
Behind this circling hiss is the rustle

Of the long-dead, whose puffed flesh once flaked
In the rubbing waters as a drawn-out whisper.
There is scratching in the storm, water
Scratching at sand, and ghost fingernails

Clawing at rock, trapped in the returning tides
Where sea-froth slaps at the cliff face, hanging
In lumps like bronchial spit turned cold.
I once saw a drowned man washed up

With this same white spit dribbling from his mouth,
Fat, like a seal cub, his sex shrivelled to a bud.
I have officiated twice
At the marriage of the dead with their sea-biers,

Scattering the surprisingly small helpings
Of musty grey ash into the sea-smell they loved –
One, my father, the other
A friend. Young deaths, seafarers both.

Storm-fish
(For my late father)

We caught the silver-sided mackerel
On spinners twisting four to a line.
The fish, translating the skipping metal as sprat,
Are hooked for their error by the lip flesh
Or the black cavity of the mouth
And swung onto deck bug-eyed, their glossed bodies
Kept moist by rain beating on the varnished deck.

A layer of spent scales, a new skin born of the dead fish
From hours of thumb and finger under brown-blooded
    gills,
Is combed from my palms in seconds
By the falling teeth of the storm, with water
Lunging under us like a green whale rising to the rain,
Ready to reclaim the stiffening fish
And barb our lungs with stinging brine.

The Sea Reclaims

The sea disgorges with a violence;
I know her ways.
She coughs up sailors wrapped in phlegm:
One is a friend recognised amongst
Her tidespill, long since licked of air.

Like him, we are salt-logged on the inner,
Once had gills and beamed with health
In the tides of the only-known sea
Where the womb's lifeline, plugged into belly,
Bobs like a water snake, its blooded mouth

Rooting in the red placental mud,
The swimmer gulping on oxides, caught
In the motion of the single wave
That breaks and delivers
High and dry on the soils of the Earth

Into folds of loam, dry rills of volcanoes,
The rucked islands white with farmers' lime,
Which the sea cannot reclaim.
Born, sitting,
Crying for the first waters.

Specimens in Resin, Specimens in Cases

As he was setting the insect in resin
He thought he could hear the singular buzz of its flight,
As if the creature had turned up the volume at its death
Of a million entrapped wingbeats clipped
By the resin cooling clear as glass.

The hum of the wingbeats grew stronger.
He eyed the specimen closely while
Sound poured from the cold round of resin
Into the cases of chloroformed moths
That lined his study, each with its
Eye-patterned wings stretched and its thorax pinned.

Their paper wings seemed to vibrate
At the same frequency as the resin-locked specimen
Until the whole room danced, and he was afloat
And crazed on the common mantra of the entombed
    insects
Singing through the windows of their wooden cases,
So that he was sure he might some day die of the noise,
Though it was an ecstasy, and amongst
The insects' tune he scratched a reminder
On paper as thin as the moths' wings
While he set about another specimen with the chloroform
    and pins:
That his coffin be lidded with glass the colour of amber.

The Storm That Hoodwinks

I. *Theory*

The man, a telescopic searcher
Bleary-eyed from looking, a cloudbuster
Fingering into weather in uncertain ways
Worrying after the deluge he has caused.

The man's body a weather tower like a lighthouse
Upping stone-stiff into cloud,
The winding stairway his stepped-up senses
That gather in deeply-bowled eyes.

The woman's body a deepwater well
With moss-soft skin polished on the inside to mirror
    finish
By the coming and going of waters
Knows the weather by touch, its timely round, its outcries.

II. *Practice*

We stand under sheet lightning, under floods of light:
God's laundry hung crackling across grey cloud
Unpacking rain in handsome loads.
While thunder claps

The rain is sustained applause,
Torrents smacking the earth.
Our clothes have caught the clap of water;
We were infected at first touch.

Devolution of Light

(A short history of the world, where horse outlives human).

I
In the beginning
The sun's sweat boils away
In its own atmosphere.
The sun ran – its legs were cut away
And the ball of the body
Bled for thousands of years

Stuck in a fixed motion
Unable to sprint from orbit,
Carrying with it nine pocked
Rocks and a belt of white-
Hot pebbles swimming
In a dry storm of meteors.

Now the small star rises
From the black tub of nightlight
And smiles over a moon-
Struck sea making pearls.

II
Birth of the Boneless Fish

Underwater celts, thunder-stones
Drawn out of their element,
Softened in brine.

The first boneless bells of jellyfish,
Packed with eyebright,
Swam in shoals to the rotten follicles

Of the sea-bed, where weed had been sucked back,
And there drew curlicues of poison
Into their oily domes, and shook out stinging tassels.

III
Some few moments ago in the history of the world
A female of the species
With a rising tide in her belly
Made certain motions that aggravated
A seed into permanent change,
Into special flesh;

And a baby whistled in the womb
Before tunes were invented;

The woman had just swung down from the trees,
Sniffing her newborn through
Shortened pig-snout.

He is born red-bearded with extra toe.

IV
Now humans have fallen by the wayside
As a successful species
And the sun is flaring wildly.

The last remaining cephalopod's bone
Is boiled white, bleached out and flaking
Like the muscle of over-cooked fish,

The shell finally drying to a powder;
Salt-white cuttlebone stranded
With other treasures worked over

By the sea, such as the world's last
Broken bottle, beached glass returning to itself
In a sisterhood of silica.

V

The scorched sand is drummed by running horses,
Hooves spinning up shell-shards, nostrils flaring
At the salt-smell of crisp, desiccate weed

And the newly-arrived odour
Of the burn of a burst sun,
Like a hot steam iron on cotton.

Dream Work

The reptile's squat eye has descended.
It is the pineal gland, senser
Of heat exchange between bodies
That is the information of attraction,
The chemistry of response.

When we fell in love, hormones scratched
On the air passed from one pineal to the other
In chains, in rope-lengths, in relative ship-loads,
Fatty acids docking at the pea-sized gland

That Descartes called the seat of the soul.
When we tested our love, the dream lost its location,
And we could not tell whether it was in, between,
Or outside us, with its piglet-squeals

And mother-in-labour cries, its laughter
Of embarrassment, and rough justice.
The pineal was jugged in its own juices
Under closed eyes, each of us at the back

Of our own faces, raising blisters, pouring balm.

Ordinary Things, Once Discovered, Never Forgotten

The shew-stone that is a black mirror
Parceled in the tight earth like a black pearl
For millenia, surfacing shiny with its history:
A lump of ordinary coal, unpacking its light to the scryer
Who in his gazing reaps the harvest
Held by the crushed bones of trees, his eyes
Sipping the jet woodgrain that lay sour for years.

The nipple-topped fungus whose musty alkaloids
Are gnomic, burrowing in the brain-stem
To spike the regular rhythms of the senses
With unnatural visions, caricaturing those normally
Suspended in the crack where day meets night,
Where space and sound unnerve the chemicals of mind
Making moonshine in the oldest established still,

A heady sourmash that restores sight to the purblind,
Distilled by Eve in the red dirt of Africa's savannah.

Wintering

In winter, it seems as if
The tongue of Cornwall is packed
In an envelope of drizzle
From tip to Tamar-throat.

The east is lined by stringy clay,
White like rennet.
The west has collapsed veins of tin,
Forgotten shoals of oily pilchard,
And the black stumps of the lost
Penzance forest, lipping
The murderous Atlantic.

But here too is silica-glass
And mica-glass tuned to the
Hum of insects in Spring;
Milk and rose quartz, spiked with static;
And after each Cornish squall
I look to the ancient barrow-heads
Haired by gorse. Open-jawed skulls
Of packed flint and crustacea;
Ghost-heads of Cornish aboriginals
Gathered in every cloud of pollen
Brushed from the yellow gorse-flower.

Bone Augury

I
Here is a bird burst open
By some misfortune, caught by
The cat's claw perhaps, its tiny,
Dark gizzards spilling from the wound.
I've hidden the bird. Its flesh
Will fall from the bones as compost,
And weather will bleach the skeleton.

II
This dawn, delicate spider-lines
Weighted by tiny beads of dew
Cling to the bright bones fallen neatly
On the earth, itself as dark as oak bark.
From the bones, ready to be stirred
Into the soil, I pick five. Delicate,
No more than an inch long, each one.
Like a child testing their worth,
I know it is right to lick each bone,
Then hold them loosely in my fist,
The edges nuzzling my flesh.
At this moment an owl flies by,
So close that I can feel the breeze
From its wingbeats on my skin.
The moon-bird is fresh from a night's hunt.
She is as white as the bones I cup.
I imagine the owl stripping flesh
From another bird spilling bruised guts,
And the five bones, flanked by my fingers,
Seem to warm and feel gently alive.

Tremedda Farm

The worst storm of the year.

Rain polishing a cobbled yard
By night; while sharp winds stitch

Bright water into the eyelets
Of the stone work, driving the rain

Into the pocks and hollows
Where the crystal shows through.

In the howling weather
A fox pads the granite.

By dawn, it is still. The slick cobble,
Spattered with a shiny green

Lard of chicken droppings,
Reflects the morning light; feathers

Festoon the yard, lumped into wet balls.
The fox, having savoured

The interior wetness of the fowl,
Lies somewhere, digesting the white meat

While the rain dries up;
His fur pearled with shining water.

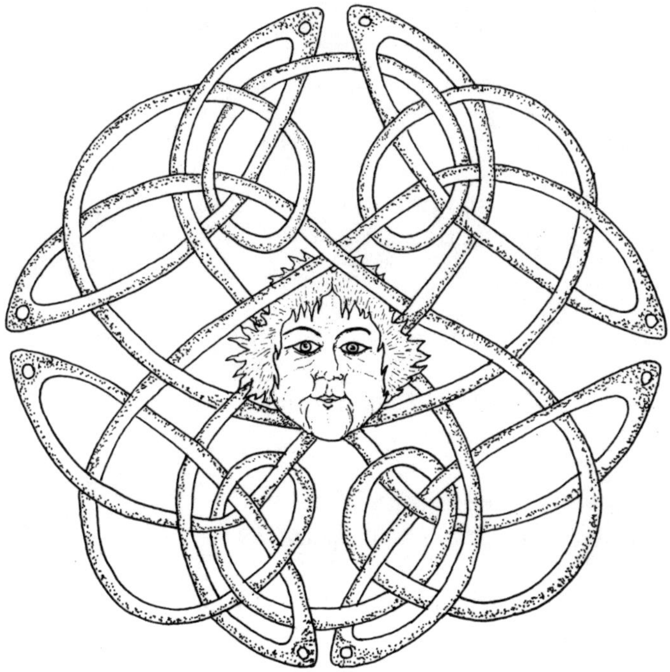